AS LIFE HAPPENS

Book of Poems

ELIJAH TAYLOR

This is a work of nonfiction poetry.
Names have been modified at the author's discretion.

Copyright © 2020 by Elijah Taylor

First paperback edition Aug 2020
First eBook edition Aug 2020

Editor, & Graphic Design: Waqas Hussain

ISBN: 978-0-578-79561-4 (paperback)
(Ebook)

www.as-life-happens.com

AUTHOR'S NOTE

Elijah Taylor is the author of "A Bottle for My Emotions." This poem was performed first at Friendship West Baptist Church. In the spring of 2020, "A Bottle for My Emotions" was published by The Beacon at Sam Houston State University. Elijah began writing poetry in 2018 as a coping mechanism for depression. The following year, Elijah joined Music Nation at Sam Houston State University. Music Nation gave Elijah a platform to share his poetry with different audiences. The Fall of 2019 Elijah performed "I Am More Than" at Music Nation's Pure Spoken Luxury.

Elijah's first poetry book "As Life Happens" was published during the COVID-19 pandemic. The major themes included in this book include love, transition, depression, and rejection. Elijah's purpose for this poetry book is to demonstrate perseverance.

SPECIAL THANKS

I would like to say thank you to everyone who helped push me to finish this book. Thank you to my mother, Cecilia Taylor. She always encouraged me to prepare for the next move. During the COVID-19 pandemic, I was able to put the finishing touches to this book. To my father, Verlin Taylor, I would like to say thank you for giving me new ideas on how to enhance my craft. To my sister, Brianna Taylor, I would like to say thank you for supporting my dream. To my aunt, Antonette Godbolt, I would like to say thank you for giving me constructive criticism and for supporting my vision. To my grandmother, Betty Taylor, I would like to say thank you for being my biggest fan.

To my favorite English 3 AP teacher, Mrs. Thornton, I would like to say thank you for teaching me the English language and for giving me a passion for writing. To my old counselor, Bonnie Baker, I would like to say thank you for your support throughout the years. To my trainer and family friend, Johnny Black, I would like to say thank you for teaching me about structure. To my old professor, Dr. Mary Petron, I would like to say thank you for encouraging me to submit my poems to The Beacon at Sam Houston State University. To my mentor and teacher, Evelyn Surgers, thank you for introducing me to the environment in which I will soon be in. To Dr. Benita Brooks, I would like to say thank you for opening new doors.

To my close friend, Claudia Ezeani, I would like to say thank you for supporting me in my poetry endeavors. To the Fall of 2018, I would like to say thank you for changing me. To my Music Nation family at Sam Houston State University, I would like to say thank you for being all ears and for introducing me to a new platform. I could not have done this without you guys and your support. I hope that everyone enjoys reading *As Life Happens*.

Robbery

"Robbery challenges me to think beyond the surface. It inspires me to look for solutions and find hope."

- Jane Thornton

Cry Like A Man

"They say real men don't cry but I say who are they. They are a lie. Because I am a REAL MAN and, in my eyes, they do cry. I am proud to see the child I knew growing into the man God called him to. Let God continue to use you and your gift of poetry to impact the world."

- Johnny Black

A Bottle For My Emotions

"Your poem actually made me cry, I thought of my son who is holding so much pain inside from his early trauma. He is a man and he will not allow himself to let it out."

- Mary Petron

Lost & Found

"The poem took me back to when I was a teenager. It is haunting yet hopeful, beautiful, and moving."

- Bonnie Baker

CONTENTS

A Bottle for My Emotions

We were taught not to feel.
Denial of expression from society has kept man from being real.
Being in tune with yourself is peace that many of us
may never feel.
A bottle for my emotions, but I never became open.
I am searching for a release, but my pride will not
allow this notion.
The weight of the world's shoulders is upon you.
Even in moments when we feel like breaking, we are
reminded we must move on.
Even in moments when life is not compensating, we are
reminded life goes on.
No stoppage or breaks when life goes wrong. A bottle for my
emotions, but I never became open.
Support for being open, but I am reminded that feelings are not
a part of my make.
I want to be open, but my mind will not allow this notion.
I fight against emotion in moments when others
witness my loss of focus.
We were never looked upon as weak, but sometimes I feel
hopeless. A bottle for my emotions, but I never became open.

The Veil of Our Fears

The fear of you knowing the real me is something
that I cannot fathom. Lack of empathy is the reason
for systematic distress. Vacancy in thy heart
stemming from uncertainty, and not
knowing what comes next.
Yearning for the confidence to face
the love that one fears.
Counsel over pessimistic thoughts that makes love feel unreal.
Acknowledging that being scared is the main reason
we try to deny.
The veil of our fears is erased when being vulnerable is fine.
Being open-minded to change is not a crime.
In order to face the veil of our fears, one must take care
of their mind.

Robbery

You are a common noun that causes great agony.

You are a catastrophe.

You divide humanity.

You make life not promising.

You are robbery.

We all know robbery oh so well.

So many stories that we can tell.

Robbery by the gun, our mothers do not feel well.

Robberies occurring because of self-hate.

Many will hate for you to make it out of your current state.

Many will plan to rob you of the picture that

they fail to paint.

There is no escape.

No matter the location of your estate.

No matter how hard you try to make love reciprocate.

There will always be another robbery that affects our mental

state.

Why do you follow me?

I cannot stand to see another robbery.

Hi Goodbye Nice To Meet You

We stare into each other eyes with a gaze that indicates one of us
better capitalize.
She has now become my state of mind
The pedestal of my demise
Like the buffet, I cannot get enough of her
Good start things end tragic
Nonresponsive and I know what happened
A push-pull factor that I cannot win
I see you as more than a friend
I chase to the end
The only problem is that there is no compromise in just being
friends
Hi Goodbye Nice to meet you.

Love

Love is a 4-letter Word
Divided by The 'OV' which symbolizes
a greater meaning. Love is most commonly mistaken
for lust. Patience is the key to true love and
happiness.
I am a victim too, of misinterpreting Love's full intentions. How
could I possibly
love someone else if I do not love myself?
My happiness seems to come and go, and I am left pondering
on my depression.
Love is a beautiful thing that connect others.
We all deserve love because a human without love would be
incomplete.
One should only embrace the aspect of love when capable of
dealing with its responsibilities.

Release

Release from the feeling of being deprived.

Release from the feeling of being neglected when direction was hard to find.

The release of voids that have devoured my time.

The release of hurt that is carved deep inside.

The release of feeling inadequate as others surpass me.

The release of low self-esteem which has kept me from shining.

Release from my greatest worries that only contemplate my lifetime.

The release of feeling hopeless as failure lingers on my mind.

Yearning to be released from depression, which has kept me from being set free.

X

Love is beautiful in its own existence, but Love is a curse when we remain to be lifted. My perception never stays consistent. I seek validation in times when I lose commitment. How did self-love become so dependent? Like a broken vase I am over the place, and I would like to be put back together.

The X stands for the unknown that we are all trying to solve. We hope to meet the expectations we set. We hope someone will help to brace our fall. We hope that people will be able to lead us to our call. We hope that the inevitable does not happen. Living life with a plan of words, but no form of action.

As we grow in age, we will experience several pains. No pain worse than the unbearable growing pains. Life is a test of perseverance and change. Our lives will never be the same. Who will remain?

Lost & Found

Reaching for purpose in a world filled with distractions.
I am my greatest enemy if I ever question my lack of passion.
The hardest part in living this life is finding means of
satisfaction.
The thought of being confident is something new to me.
My counterfeit could never portray who I desired to be.
The thought of being lost without vision is something that I
cannot unsee.
A battle between progression and regression.
A battle between learning or disregarding previous lessons
A battle between staying true when life becomes blue.

I Am

I am a Black man living in the 21st century.

The embodiment of prosperity I long for.

I wonder if I am equipped to live the American Dream.

I desire to make a difference before I depart from the Earth.

I worry that the youth of today will struggle to embrace their worth.

I am uncertain this applies to me.

I m a Black man living in the 21st century.

I battle trauma that cannot be hidden.

I despise the intelligence that I have been given.

I contemplate wanting to be driven.

I fear progress being disrespect.

My downfall is not knowing what is best.

I am a Black man living in the 21st Century.

Where progress is not always what it seems.

I am now capable of achieving what was laid before me.

I am my ancestor's wildest dreams.

These pages will not go foreseen.

I am a Black man living in the 21st Century.

8 AM

8 A.M.
5'7".
Skinny.
Brown-skinned.

Blue Nike hoodie.
Very aloof.
Incredibly quiet.

I stare from my wing.
I look away if you peep.
I want you close to me.

I See You

I see her early.
Forget Philosophy.
It's 8 A.M.

Have you seen me before.
I caught you staring.
Your name is
Elijah, right?
Yeah
Your name is
Your name is Cierra, right?
Yes.

You're cute.
I think you're cute, too.
Can I get to know you?
Sure, why not.
What is your number?
832-***-***

We should hang out sometime.
Sit by me tomorrow.

The End

To the world, I could not see.
Being the man of your dreams, I could not be.
If only I could lead.

Stimulate

I hope that we can stimulate each other beyond measures that our soul can take.
Because no one likes the feeling of always having to contemplate.
I hope that we truly do relate.
Loving is not easy, but with the right person we could all find the true meaning.
When I say 'stimulate,' I am not just referring to the physical realm.
I need conversation.
When I say stimulate, I am referring to the quirk that you continue to hide.
I desire to be intrigued
With conversation that ponders after time.
What is life without sublime?

I Am More Than

I am more than a temporary quick fix.
Or a temporary sensation that is either a hit or miss.
Or a toy that you can throw away day to day at your own dismay.
I am more than a puppet in which you hold the strings.
My heart cannot be tampered with, as you dangle me amongst many things.

I am more than an appointment.
I am more than an account.
I am more than a listening ear.
I am more than a zone, in which you believe that I may never clear.
I am more than a bench warmer whom may never enter the game.

I am a man that deserves many things.
I am more than your midnight teaser or morning pleaser.
I am a Man.

Tight Squeeze

The transition from boy to man is a complex squeeze.
Enclosed by life's pressure, I struggle to breathe.
Maybe I am not Ford-tough after all.
Life gives two options.
Continue to climb or you will not prevail.

I knew that one day I would grow.
I was unaware when that day would be.
My mindset changed and life changed accordingly.
Memories remind me of who I once was.
I then realized life cannot be recaptured from the past.

When I was a child, I spoke like a child.
Thought like a child.
Reasoned like a child.
When I became a man, I gave away childish things.

Love Me

These two words are desperation.
These two words are incarceration.
I never thought I would rehearse these words to you.
I hoped you would know what to do.

Love Me
Insecurities in all.
Imperfections in all.
Do not add to my pain.
I am tired of seeing rain.
Love Me

If you awaken my heart, that is all that I expect.
If your feelings change, I hope you will project.
Will you soften the blow until we have completed the
transaction?
This is my final call and plan of action.
Love Me

Cry Like A Man

I was told to never let tears fall from your eyes.
A mask is the perfect disguise.
My emotions stay on the backburner.
I contemplate how I will survive without prior knowledge of
being alive.
You are a natural release, but I hesitate if I should ever let you
leave.
I am ashamed of your nature as you leave me vulnerable to
bleed.

When you fall from my eye
I quickly wipe you.
The slightest sign of weakness, my ego cannot take.
I am entrapped in tears hoping they will flow.
I am in bondage, and I am praying to be set free.

I wish my emotions were not soft spoken.
Tears roll down from my eyes as pain is released from my soul.
I am not weak, but these tears help me to gain control.

Dear Anxiety

Shaking uncontrollably, I hate how you make me feel.
Wondering what has come over me.
I cannot stand still.
You apply pressure, hoping that I will break.
You remind me of the past in moments when I try to escape.
You are the worry that makes my heart shake.

Mental Health

Looking out for me.
I do not want harm.
I have caused myself enough damage.
Tired of being disturbed.
Tired of not having peace and not being heard.
Do you understand my guard is up?
I cannot let loose anymore.

I am only trying to maintain.
Trying to make the most out of my days.
It is a process.

Sad face.
Remove that pitiful look off your face.
It takes time.

Please understand.
I have triggers.
I have moments when I need to escape.
I will not partake.

Prescribed

A dose of anxiety.
Insurmountable stress.
A breakdown at my job.
Prescribed.

Stress lowered.
Mental intact.
Retained focus.
Sign me up.

Each morning
I often forgot to take you.
To be on-edge was the opposite of what you advertised.

Still sad.
Still stressed.
Not working, are you?

One twist of the capsule, I place you back inside.
I do not need you.
Dependent upon a supplement, I do not think so.
Placebo I need my money back.

New to Driving

They try to determine the speed in which I should live.
The fast lane for the fast drivers.
The right lane for the slow drivers.
The middle lane for those who are accustomed to change.

You either drive well or you do not.
The drivers behind you will let you know.
One honk of the car if I do not gas up at the right time.
One glare if I do not turn up or beat it.

Mr. or Mrs. Impatient did not give me room if I hit the brakes.
We are not moving now, wait!

On This Sunday

I was told to speed up.
I slightly tap the gas to satisfy my evaluator.
On this Sunday, I experience my first encounter with the law.

Hands on the steering wheel, they were not.
They were in my lap.
In that moment I forgot the cardinal rule.
In that moment I knew I screwed up.
In that moment, my fate was not in my hands.

The offense: speeding.
For some odd reason I was calm.
I did not worry about danger I worried about church.
This Sunday, God had me covered!

Two Taps

Two Taps from God on my shoulder.
Those taps were designed to carry me over.
I have been given grace.
I have been given composure.
I could not be the fuel to her fire, so we're both in better spaces
now.
God saved me and I will not forsake Him now.

Withdrawal on heavy.
Withdrawal on high.
I am learning how to survive without a woman by my side.

I am now quenched.
When I feel lonely, I am heard.
When I am distracted, I am guided by God's word.

Darkest Hour

Blinds closed.

Bad thoughts transpire.

I am accompanied by bad memories on repeat.

These memories come with vengeance.

Sleep deprived with fear inside.

I toss and turn until the awakening of sun rise.

Fetal Position

I lay in the fetal position.
Tears drench my pillowcase.
2 out of 7 days I sleep.
My mind is tired.
It spins like a rollercoaster with no end.
I would choke this hole if I could grasp it.
Drool with no care I cannot obtain.

Generational Curse

Once misguided.
Very ignorant.
Purpose snatched.
Permanent damage.
We all pay.

The mistake is noticeable.
I have made the same.
I chose the negative energy.
I chose not to turn the page.

Tied to old lies.
Tied to old ways of thinking.
Tied to a broken existence.
My family.
My pride.
That was all I knew.

As Life Changes

My old habits deteriorate.
My mind becomes new.
I gain a new sense of identity.
As life changes, I am humbled.
I learn the difference between being prideful and steadfast.
I do not engage in conversations that serve me no purpose.
As life changes, I learn the importance of fortitude.
As life changes, I stand firm.
I accept change.
I adapt to unforgiving circumstances.
I carry on.
As life changes, I prepare for the next move.

What is Love?

I am unsure if I can accurately answer.
I lack experience.
I go no further than 'situation-ships', and one relationship.
If love is kind, why can't I determine the two?

Love happens to be a comparison.
Often love is a false perception.
Love is blind to those unaware.
If love is kind, why do few share?

Love seems to be a genuine connection
Two people, one direction.
Their common goal is compassion.
Love What's Happening?

Love is power and unity.
Love is all we need.
Despite failed attempts
Love is all the heart desires.
Love is the precursor, waiting for input.
Love is just a thought for now.

Altar Call

For the sick, I am called.
Down the pew, I proceed
To a life-changing experience.

Snotty-nosed
I shake and tremble.
I know that God and courage led me here.
Fear could not change this much needed moment.

I am not alone.
My left and right wants to change as well.
I may or may not know you but in some way we relate.

Hands held.
Hands squeezed.
We pray for our days.
We pray for our neighbor's needs.

This Walk

This walk is not easy.
This walk gives life meaning.
This walk is not for the weak.
This walk is not cheap.

My life given.
My pride erased.
I could not save face.

Tight rope.
I do not control this relationship.
Side to side, I do not know what to make of it.
I may accompany death today.

Each step with precision.
Each step with dedication.
Adjacent.
No longer vacant.
This walk has taught me great patience.

Peace

I search for you in all the wrong places.
Lowest of the lows, I feel vacant.
My heart posture shows my desperation.

Outlet

Soul searching for a solution
I slipped upon poetry.
With no standard form or guidelines, I vividly express.

Emotions spill between these lines.
No longer protected
No longer terrified
My safe haven displays the burdens that I have carried over
time.

Soul Ties

Long overdue, but I am still tied to you.
Love you I told.
Many mistakes I hold.
Split we ended.
The ripping away of souls.

Tied to you baby like glue.
One glance at your necklace
Closed draw it goes.

My Elijah, you said.
We fed ducks; I ran.
Tied to you, Ms. Dash. what do I do?

Tied to your hug.
Tied to your kiss.
Tied to your passion, as it never missed.

Cannot erase my first.
Cannot erase time.
Cannot erase you.
Tied to you.

Business with Pleasure

Hardheaded, I mixed them twice.
Feelings involved, never thought twice.
My gut said otherwise.
I still had to have her.

At your service.
Hoping you would select me.
Hoping to be seen by you.

Look at you.
Look at you.
You are nice.

On the receiving end for me
Are feelings to hold.
You have grown cold.

My feelings show.
The customers know.
I cannot hide how I feel.
Eyes the other way they should have stayed.

Open Book

Enough.
Or perhaps too little.
I never know until it is too late.
I have not learned.

I peel layers back.
I talk your ears off.
I just want to be heard.

Forget a development.
Forget waiting.
This is me.
What are we waiting for?

I never shut up.
I talk too much.
I ruin chances.
My heart I give to soon.
My pages turn too quick.

Move seen checkmate.
Next line she heard.
No puzzle pieces.
No mystery to her.

Lost Files

I once wanted you.
I knew you would never leave.
Too much time shared.

At rest
You never could be.
You would hate to be deleted.
You hope I will download again.

Best of friends.
Best of the same.
I never changed.
Until the very end.

Change You

Hammer.
Tape.
I have to reconstruct.
Until you are perfect.
You may never reach this capacity.

Quite rude.
Quite inconsiderate.
The heart knows what it wants.
It beats for preference.
The heart knows this will be complicated.

Erase marks down your face.
The image in my head, I need.
I need you to change.
Fill this tailored shoe size.
Fulfill my fantasy.

Change Me

You are too sensitive.
I do not like that.
Change it.

You are very black.
Blacker than my shirt.
Change it.

You appeal to my eyes.
No physical given.
Change it.

Too calm.
Too at peace.
Or at least that is what it seems.
Change it.

You see consequences.
You do not see a good time.
You see dark places.
Change it.

Barber change.
Wardrobe change.
Voice change.
I do not like what I see.
Change it.

Moving on.
Moving forward.
Moving into self.
No backwards rotation.
Change it.

Surrender

Physical needed I got.
Accessible when needed.
Heart broken.
Deception formed.
Sex.
The basis of my relationships.

Once needed.
On edge, I need you.
How we relate.
You are my escape.
My escape from harsh realities.
I never thought you would damage me.

Flashbacks to love and pain.
A different side of me.
Thirsty for more.
Fulfilled
Never.
I want more.

Temptation creeps.
Highlights repeat.
The opportunity awaits.
My control dictates.

Fly at the Barbecue

Flags fly with no repercussions.
Statues stand high.
Liberty on standby.
Bodies drop like flies.

They let it rip like target practice.
Their body cams inactive.
Now active.

I step outside.
Not knowing if I will go back in.
They let their example be made.
I cannot digest.
To rest your allegiance.

Skittles in my hands.
My house protruded.
On the pavement I lay.
Hate crimes and paid leave.
Tired of being treated like a fly at the barbecue.

Give Me Your Card

Hand it over.
You do not represent us well.
We on go.
You do not sip red Kool-Aid.
You not Black.

You cry too much.
You not tough.
You care too much.
Throw your heart away.

Change your voice.
You are too proper.
I need to hear more cursing from your mouth.
You are better right?
More like me, you need to be.
Do not overstep me.

Coon Jr

I do not mean to be emotionless.
I do not mean to be detached.
I only know how to stay composed.
Problem spotted.
You are too peaceful.
No fire or rage.
You do not throw hands.
You are a weird specimen.
We do not rock with you.
Beat it.

Less confrontation.
More peace.
You know what times we in?
I do.
You do not.
I do.
You do not.
Less talking.
More haymakers.
People should not fight.
Well, people should not be racist.
They should not, but do you have the answer?
No solution, I thought so.
Peace Treaty Looking Ahh.

Exhibit A of a weak Black man.
Wave your hand, you sellout.

Halfway Black.
Black enough to be called purple.
My gums are black.
My teeth are white.
Appearance up.
He cares about himself.
Another instance of care shown.
Uppity.
Guess what?
I do not respect you.
You are soft.
No backbone.
How can I trust you?

You are a disgrace.
Ball up your fist.
Show me your stripes.
Show me you are a Black man.
I know you will not.
You are the definition of a coward.
You waiting to boil?
Save it.
They are seeing stars.
I do not care.

Diffuse what?
That is weak.
Not enough excitement.
I want to be riled up.

I forgot your passive, like Martin Luther King.
Difference made.
Lie down, you got to be kidding.
Nah, I do not agree.
I know bullets fly.
I know they need no reason.
I know about innocent death.
I still believe in more love, more peace.

Why trade bodies?
Why put others through more trauma and pain?
This world is sick.
I pray.
Stop with all that peaceful talk.
New level, right?
Do as I say.
Be more Black.
More Black and less peace.
Potentially.
I do not like taking risk.
More Black more we can relate.
I relate differently.
I know.
The house is calling your name.

Body Language

She has never told me she likes me.
Her body language says otherwise.
Arms not crossed.
She touches me excessively.
Elated best describes how I feel.

I like to be touched.
I like to be touched by you.
That touch leaves me mesmerized.
Daydreaming and thinking if this could be.

I watch for signs.
I study.
However, I do not know if you are fronting.
Your language speaks, but it could mean nothing.
To your body language I pay close attention.

This language is subtle.
Discrete are the actions.
Her body language speaks to me.
I am unaware if she likes me.

I Sip, I Compromise

Backwards.
Renege.
One second.
One moment.
Will not hurt.
I sip.
I compromise.
I will show you.
No square.
No weenie.
No wuss.
I am not what you think.

I sip.
I compromise.
This one time.
Will this change your mind?

For some odd reason.
Your opinion matters.
I care what you think.
You matter
Too much to me.

To Be

To be the man of your dreams.

Or the man that you tell to exit your face.

I could be both.

Depending upon my wordplay.

Depending upon if I am able to seal the deal.

Love on Repeat

Records spin.
Pictures flaunt.
I notice you every day.
I want it.
I do not know
What it takes.

It hints at maybe.
It hints at now.
If two are ready.

Love, so powerful.
Love, so drifting.
Love, so swifting.
It never stays away.

Love on my heart.
Love on my mind.
Love on my soul.
Love now, that's power control.

Love makes the heart beat.
Love makes the harp sing.
Love never misses a beat.
Love is always on repeat.

I Would Rather

I would rather express than suppress.
In tune?
Know what to do.
What not to do.
Rational, not irritational.

Tempted to be open.
One step towards closure.
Remain open? That is the question.
Soft like tissue, I would rather not be.
The real me they will not see.

I only know tough.
Oblivious to the façade.
I have never seen or heard of being in-tune.

I am a mess.
I am stressed.
I do not even know that I am depressed.
On the fence, with my greatest threat.

Emotionally Unavailable

She is used to suppression.
She is used to manipulation.
She is used to brothers that only make complications.
Cold like water, her soul turns.
Never the same, her heart burns.
She is unaware if love will share its turn.

Emotionally Unavailable

Broken.
Early.
I need no fixing.
I will not change for you.
I will not be vulnerable for you.

Open for you or not.
The field is what I am most accustomed to.
I have a life to live.
I will not settle until I am ready.

You are not the one.
It will not happen.
Sorry, I cannot be your Prince Charming.

86

Not today, I do not want it.
On the side will be fine.
Not this time.
I need a substitution.

86 how I feel.
86 Delilah.
86 sub-sensitivity for hardness.
86 my kindness.
86 ready.
86 sub you for me.

Damaged Goods

I do not want love.

I do not want connection.

I just want protection.

Feelings in a backpack.

Zip Up.

Damaged to the core.

My soul misaligns.

My heart resides in various locations.

Pity party.

I feel sorry.

Me & Dad

My real father
My real father
Said he feels like a stepfather.
We share the same name.
We share the same birthmark.
Our bond has a strain.
Divorce is our catalyst.
Divorce is our pain.
I view him differently.

Never been a hand-thrower.
Today I will.
No thought of losing.
Bro has to know how I feel.
The sleeping drill.

Why bother.
Awkward.
Silence.
Mundane.
Needed talks subside.
On your side.
I stay on my side.
Easier when we played catch.
Dads with their sons.
I wish
I could have that.

Dad Cry

Never seen Dad cry.
Never seen emotion.
Angry sometimes.
I have never seen hurt.

You would hate to be seen as weak.
You hide those emotions.
The Black generational teaching.
I know you are hurting.
I know.
You do not fool me.

You escape.
You find your outlet.
Whether it be positive or negative.
I cry.
You stop it.
You let me cry.
I will let you do what you chose not to do.